This book has been
donated by the
2000/2001 WTHS PTO
In memory of the life of
Jason Beiner

the subway series

The Yankees, the Mets and a Season to Remember

The Official Commemorative
of the 2000 World Series

The SportingNews

PHOTO CREDITS

Cover photos—*main:* Brad Mangin/MLB Photos, *from left:* Bob Leverone/The Sporting News, Albert Dickson/The Sporting News, Ron Vesely/MLB Photos, Michael Zagaris/MLB Photos, Rich Pilling/MLB Photos. **Back cover photo**—Rich Pilling/MLB Photos. **Dustjacket photo**—Albert Dickson/The Sporting News. **Pages 2-3**—Brad Mangin/MLB Photos. **5**—*counterclockwise from top:* Rich Pilling/MLB Photos, Allen Kee/MLB Photos, John Dunn for The Sporting News, Ron Vesely/MLB Photos, Ron Vesely/MLB Photos, Rich Pilling/MLB Photos, Michael Zagaris/MLB Photos. **7**—Mark Levine/MLB Photos. **8**—New York City Mayor's Photo Unit. **9**—Rich Pilling/MLB Photos. **10-11**—Rich Pilling/MLB Photos. **12-13**—Brad Mangin/MLB Photos. **14-15**—John Dunn for The Sporting News. **16-17**—*top left:* Brad Mangin/MLB Photos, *all others:* Rich Pilling/MLB Photos. **18-19**—both photos by Rich Pilling/MLB Photos. **20-21**—*clockwise from top left:* John Dunn for The Sporting News, Fred Vuich/MLB Photos, Rich Pilling/MLB Photos, Rich Pilling/MLB Photos, Rich Pilling/MLB Photos, John Dunn for The Sporting News. **22-23**—*clockwise from top left:* Rich Pilling/MLB Photos, John Dunn for The Sporting News, Dilip Vishwanat/TSN, Rich Pilling/MLB Photos, Michael Zagaris/MLB Photos, Rich Pilling/MLB Photos, Rich Pilling/MLB Photos. **24-25**—both photos by Rich Pilling/MLB Photos. **26-27**—Allen Kee/MLB Photos. **28-29**—*clockwise from top left:* Don Smith/MLB Photos, Rich Pilling/MLB Photos, Rich Pilling/MLB Photos, Steve Green/MLB Photos. **30-31**—*top left:* Allen Kee/MLB Photos, *bottom left:* Rich Pilling/MLB Photos, *right:* Brad Mangin/MLB Photos. **32-33**—Brad Mangin/MLB Photos. **34-35**—*left:* Allen Kee/MLB Photos, *top center:* Rich Pilling/MLB Photos, *bottom center:* Allen Kee/MLB Photos, *right:* Allen Kee/MLB Photos. **36-37**—*clockwise from top left:* Allen Kee/MLB Photos, Steve Green/MLB Photos, Michael Zagaris/MLB Photos, John Reid III/MLB Photos, Allen Kee/MLB Photos. **38-39**—*clockwise from top left:* John Williamson/MLB Photos, Allen Kee/MLB Photos, Rich Pilling/MLB Photos, Brad Mangin/MLB Photos, John Williamson/MLB Photos, Michael Zagaris/MLB Photos, Rich Pilling/MLB Photos, Rich Pilling/MLB Photos. **40-41**—*clockwise from top left:* Rich Pilling/MLB Photos, Rich Pilling/MLB Photos, Rich Pilling/MLB Photos, Rich Pilling/MLB Photos, Brad Mangin/MLB Photos, Rich Pilling/MLB Photos. **42-43**—*counterclockwise from top left:* Rich Pilling/MLB Photos, Rich Pilling/MLB Photos, Rich Pilling/MLB Photos, John Dunn for The Sporting News, Rich Pilling/MLB Photos, Robert Seale/The Sporting News, Bob Leverone/The Sporting News, George Tiedemann/MLB Photos. **44-45**—both photos by Mark Levine/MLB Photos. **46-47**—all photos by Bob Leverone/The Sporting News. **48-49**—Ezra Shaw/Allsport. **50-51**—all photos by Rich Pilling/MLB Photos. **52-53**—both photos by Michael Zagaris/MLB Photos. **54-55**—Michael Zagaris/MLB Photos. **56-57**—all photos by Rich Pilling/MLB Photos. **58-59**—both photos by John Dunn for The Sporting News. **60-61**—both photos by Michael Zagaris/MLB Photos. **62-63**—*main:* Paul Nisely/The Sporting News, *inset:* Albert Dickson/The Sporting News. **64-65**—*left:* Paul Nisely/The Sporting News, *main:* Paul Nisely/The Sporting News, *top right:* Albert Dickson/The Sporting News, *center right:* Albert Dickson/The Sporting News, *bottom right:* Paul Nisely/The Sporting News. **66-67**—*main:* Albert Dickson/The Sporting News, *top right:* Albert Dickson/The Sporting News, *bottom right:* Peter Newcomb/The Sporting News. **68-69**—*top row left to right:* Albert Dickson/The Sporting News, Peter Newcomb/The Sporting News, Albert Dickson/The Sporting News, Albert Dickson/The Sporting News, Albert Dickson/The Sporting News, Albert Dickson/The Sporting News, Albert Dickson/The Sporting News; *center row left to right:* Albert Dickson/The Sporting News, Albert Dickson/The Sporting News, Albert Dickson/The Sporting News, Albert Dickson/The Sporting News; *bottom row left to right:* Dilip Vishwanat/The Sporting News, Albert Dickson/The Sporting News, Albert Dickson/The Sporting News. **70-71**—Rich Pilling/MLB Photos. **72-73**—*top row left to right:* Rich Pilling/MLB Photos, Rich Pilling/MLB Photos, Rich Pilling/MLB Photos, Rich Pilling/MLB Photos, Rich Pilling/MLB Photos; *center row left to right:* Bob Leverone/The Sporting News, Bob Leverone/The Sporting News, Bob Leverone/The Sporting News, Rich Pilling/MLB Photos, Bob Leverone/The Sporting News; *bottom row left to right:* Bob Leverone/The Sporting News, Bob Leverone/The Sporting News, Bob Leverone/The Sporting News. **74-75**—*top to bottom:* Rich Pilling/MLB Photos, Rich Pilling/MLB Photos, Bob Leverone/The Sporting News; *main:* John Dunn for The Sporting News. **76-77**—*clockwise from left:* Bob Leverone/The Sporting News, Bob Leverone/The Sporting News, Rich Pilling/MLB Photos, Bob Leverone/The Sporting News, Rich Pilling/MLB Photos, Rich Pilling/MLB Photos. **78-79**—Bob Leverone/The Sporting News. **80-81**—all photos by Bob Leverone/The Sporting News. **82-82**—all photos by John Dunn for The Sporting News. **84-85**—all photos by John Dunn for The Sporting News. **86-87**—all photos by John Dunn for The Sporting News. **88-89**—all photos by John Dunn for The Sporting News. **90-91**—both photos by Robert Seale/The Sporting News. **92-93**—all photos by Robert Seale/The Sporting News. **94-95**—all photos by Robert Seale/The Sporting News. **96-97**—all photos by Robert Seale/The Sporting News. **98-99**—all photos by Robert Seale/The Sporting News. **100-101**—all photos by Robert Seale/The Sporting News. **102-103**—all photos by Rich Pilling/MLB Photos. **104-105**—all photos by Rich Pilling/MLB Photos. **106-107**—*main:* George Tiedemann/MLB Photos; all other photos by Ron Vesely/MLB Photos. **108-109**—Albert Dickson/The Sporting News. **110-111**—*top row left to right:* Robert Seale/The Sporting News, John Dunn for The Sporting News, Albert Dickson/The Sporting News, Albert Dickson/The Sporting News, Ron Vesely/MLB Photos; *center row:* both photos by Albert Dickson/The Sporting News; *bottom row:* both photos by John Dunn for The Sporting News. **112-113**—*clockwise from left:* Albert Dickson/The Sporting News, Albert Dickson/The Sporting News, Albert Dickson/The Sporting News, Robert Seale/The Sporting News. **114-115**—*clockwise from top left:* Albert Dickson/The Sporting News, Ron Vesely/MLB Photos, Ron Vesely/MLB Photos, Ron Vesely/MLB Photos, Albert Dickson/The Sporting News, Robert Seale/The Sporting News. **116-117**—*left to right:* Ron Vesely/MLB Photos, Robert Seale/The Sporting News, Ron Vesely/MLB Photos, Robert Seale/The Sporting News. **118-119**—*clockwise from bottom left:* Ron Vesely/MLB Photos, Robert Seale/The Sporting News, Robert Seale/The Sporting News, Ron Vesely/MLB Photos, Albert Dickson/The Sporting News, Ron Vesely/MLB Photos. **120-121**—*clockwise from top left:* Ron Vesely/MLB Photos, Ron Vesely/MLB Photos, Ron Vesely/MLB Photos, Ron Vesely/MLB Photos, Albert Dickson/The Sporting News, Robert Seale/The Sporting News, Robert Seale/The Sporting News, Ron Vesely/MLB Photos, Albert Dickson/The Sporting News. **122-123**—*clockwise from top left:* Ron Vesely/MLB Photos, Robert Seale/The Sporting News, Albert Dickson/The Sporting News, Albert Dickson/The Sporting News, Ron Vesely/MLB Photos, Ron Vesely/MLB Photos, Ron Vesely/MLB Photos, Ron Vesely/MLB Photos. **124-125**—Robert Seale/The Sporting News. **126-127**—*clockwise from top left:* Robert Seale/The Sporting News, John Dunn for The Sporting News, Albert Dickson/The Sporting News, Robert Seale/The Sporting News. **128-129**—*clockwise from top left:* Albert Dickson/The Sporting News, Robert Seale/The Sporting News, Robert Seale/The Sporting News, John Dunn for The Sporting News. **130-131**—*clockwise from left:* John Dunn for The Sporting News, Albert Dickson/The Sporting News, John Dunn for The Sporting News, Robert Seale/The Sporting News, Albert Dickson/The Sporting News. **132-133**—*main:* Robert Seale/The Sporting News, *top right:* John Dunn for The Sporting News, *bottom right:* Albert Dickson. **134-135**—all photos by John Dunn for The Sporting News. **136-137**—*clockwise from top left:* John Dunn for The Sporting News, Robert Seale/The Sporting News, John Dunn for The Sporting News, John Dunn for The Sporting News, Robert Seale/The Sporting News. **138-139**—*clockwise from top left:* Robert Seale/The Sporting News, John Dunn for The Sporting News, Robert Seale/The Sporting News, Robert Seale/The Sporting News, Albert Dickson/The Sporting News. **140-141**—John Dunn for The Sporting News. **142-143**—*left:* John Dunn for The Sporting News, *top right:* John Dunn for The Sporting News, *bottom right:* Robert Seale/The Sporting News. **144-145**—*top left:* Robert Seale/The Sporting News, *top right:* Albert Dickson/The Sporting News, *main:* John Dunn for The Sporting News. **146-147**—*main:* Robert Seale/The Sporting News, *counterclockwise from top left:* Brad Mangin/MLB Photos, John Dunn for The Sporting News, John Dunn for The Sporting News, Albert Dickson/The Sporting News, Robert Seale/The Sporting News. **148-149**—*counterclockwise from left:* Brad Mangin/MLB Photos, Brad Mangin/MLB Photos, Rich Pilling/MLB Photos, Rich Pilling/MLB Photos, Albert Dickson/The Sporting News. **150-151**—*clockwise from top left:* Brad Mangin/MLB Photos, Rich Pilling/MLB Photos, Rich Pilling/MLB Photos, Albert Dickson/The Sporting News, Albert Dickson/The Sporting News, Albert Dickson/The Sporting News, Rich Pilling/MLB Photos.

CONTENTS

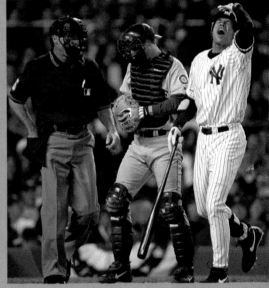

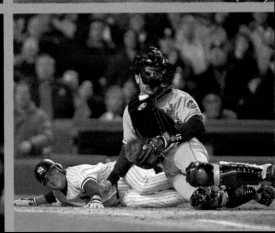

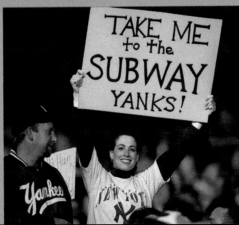

the SUBWAY SERIES

The Yankees, the Mets and a Season to Remember

The Official Commemorative of the 2000 World Series

Editorial Director
Steve Meyerhoff

Art Directors
Bob Parajon
Bill Wilson

Design and Production
Chris Barnes
Dave Brickey
Michael Behrens
Matt Kindt
Angie Pillman
Steve Romer
Christen Sager

Director of Photography
Fred Barnes

Photographers
Albert Dickson
Bob Leverone
Robert Seale
Dilip Vishwanat

Editorial Assistance
Matt Crossman
Rob Rains
Ron Smith
David Walton

Produced in partnership and licensed by
MAJOR LEAGUE BASEBALL PROPERTIES, INC.

Executive Vice President
Timothy J. Brosnan

Senior Director of Publishing
Donald S. Hintze

Editor
Michael J. McCormick

Manager, MLB Photos
Rich Pilling

Administrator, MLB Photos
Paul Cunningham

Acknowledgements

A mere listing of names cannot begin to express the level of commitment this group of people dedicated to this project. We share a passion for baseball and for words and pictures. When all of them come together, this becomes more than just a job.

Evenso, there was a lot of work involved in getting this project completed quickly and with the highest quality we expect in our books. Bob Parajon, The Sporting News' prepress director, took on the role of art director, overseeing the design and production and photo editing of the book. The fact that the production of this book coincided with turning back the clocks one hour only gave Bob an extra hour to work. Special thanks to Bob's family and especially his wife, Andrea, who "postponed" their 10th wedding anniversary to get this book out on time. Bob, you're our MVP.

You'll no doubt note the outstanding pictures that tell the stories of the Mets' and Yankees' seasons in this book, from the regular season to the final out of the Subway Series. A group of photographers from The Sporting News, under the direction of Fred Barnes, who edited countless rolls of their film, showed their extraordinary talent once again: thank you Albert Dickson, Bob Leverone, Robert Seale and Dilip Vishwanat. Thank you, too, to the talented photographers of Major League Baseball, led by friend and former colleague Rich Pilling. You have left us with lasting images of the season.

Thanks to The Sporting News prepress staff—Chris Barnes, Dave Brickey and Steve Romer—whose work scanning and color-correcting images always amazes me. I always think I've seen your best work yet, then you do even better on the next project.

When it comes to words, The Sporting News' Ron Smith always has a way with them, as his telling accounts of the postseason games attest. Thanks to Rob Rains, who dropped everything to write season reviews not just for the Mets and Yankees that appear in this book, but for two other teams as well just in case we would need them.

Thanks, too, to those who brought the words and pictures together: Bill Wilson, Angie Pillman and Michael Behrens.

You are a talented group of people and you should be proud for what you've accomplished.

The Sporting News is a registered trademark of The Sporting News, a division of Vulcan Print Media, Inc. Visit our website at www.sportingnews.com

ISBN: 0-89204-659-7 (softcover)
ISBN: 0-89204-658-9 (hardcover)

Introduction

It began long before the first pitch from Andy Pettitte to Timo Perez in the first game of the World Series, long before Tino Martinez squeezed a throw from Derek Jeter to set up the Mets-Yankees Subway Series showdown.

No, this Subway Series began more than three months earlier, on a warm Saturday afternoon just before the All-Star break.

Because of a rainout earlier in the season, a modification had to be made to the regular-season schedule, a modification that would create on July 8, 2000, a home-and-home day-night doubleheaders in the same city in different ballparks, first in Shea Stadium and then in Yankee Stadium.

In and of itself, the doubleheader was an event to remember. Dwight Gooden took the mound at Shea, just like the old days ... except this time he was wearing Yankee colors. A controversial obstruction call heats things up as the Yankees win the opener, 4-2.

But it's only the beginning.

In a second game, Yankees starter Roger Clemens hits Mets catcher Mike Piazza in the head with a pitch. Words ensue. Accusations are exchanged. Yankees win again, 4-2.

Again, it's only the beginning ...

Dwight Gooden took the mound as a Yankee during a July game at Shea.

Foreword

by Mayor Rudy Giuliani

Yogi Berra, Joe DiMaggio, Whitey Ford and Mickey Mantle. That's not just a list of some of the greatest baseball players ever to play the game, those are the players I grew up cheering for. They were Yankees.

My father's love for the Yankees was passed on to me in what would have been a natural development in a father-son relationship, if not for a couple of interesting factors: First, my mother and her side of the family were life-long Dodgers fans; second, we lived a mile from Ebbets Field, right in the heart of Dodger country.

I grew up as a Yankee fan in the most hostile of environments; that instilled character. And I grew up during the heyday of the Subway Series; that instilled a love for the game that filled every April with promise, and every October with excitement.

From 1949 through 1958, every World Series involved at least one team from New York City. It was a way of life. Most Octobers, the City's neighborhoods and families were divided. In 1949, 1952, 1953, 1955 and 1956, the City was gripped by a Yankees-Dodgers series. During three of those series, the prospect of Game 7 hypnotized New York City. Every fan held his or her breath for 24 hours. In two of the three seventh games, Yankees fans exhaled with joy. And after the 1955 Game 7 Dodgers victory, my mother's side of the family was finally vindicated.

In the 1956 Subway Series, the Yankees went ahead three games to two against the Dodgers when Don Larsen pitched his perfect game. The game marked the culmination—and captured all of the excitement—of the Subway Series era. Two days later, the Yankees won Game 7, 9-0, and that era came to an end.

For more than four decades, our City didn't enjoy even the prospect of a Subway Series. First, we lost the Dodgers and the Giants in one fell swoop in 1957. Then, after New York City gained the Mets in 1962, the Yankees and Mets didn't make the postseason in the same year until 1999.

From 1957 through 1999, the Yankees brought home eight World Series titles. The Mets brought home two thrilling championships, including the Miracle Mets' victory in 1969 and the dramatic 1986 comeback win over Boston. But a few things were missing from those 10 titles: the thrill of a city coming together and then being divided, cross-town rivals looking each other in the eye and the exaltation that goes with bragging rights in the greatest city in the world.

The 1997 season whetted the appetite of New Yorkers for another Subway Series, when the Mets and the Yankees met for the first time during interleague play. During that year's three-game series, the City felt the magic of a regular-season Subway Series. Over a 162-game schedule, three games may seem inconsequential, but it got cross-town rivals to meet face-to-face and put bragging rights up for grabs. In 1997 the Yankees won those rights, two games to one.

Interleague play has brought the Yankees and Mets together 18 times. The Yankees have won the majority of those regular-season battles, but each one has been hard-fought, and in many cases the score has been close.

Four years of interleague play has produced plenty of drama, but the day that came the closest to capturing the spirit of the Subway Series era was the historic day-night doubleheader on July 8th of this year. For the first time since 1903, two New York teams played two games in two different stadiums in one day. It was part of a four-game series, and our City was gripped by the showdown. Just like during the Subway Series era, fan loyalty divided workplaces, neighborhoods and households. Subway platforms, diners and the media were filled with debate about who was the best hitter, which team had the best pitching and what it would take for one team to win in the other's stadium.

Orlando Hernandez won a close game in the series opener, 2-1. In the day game of the doubleheader, Dwight Gooden made a triumphant return to Shea Stadium and earned the win as a Yankee. In the night game, Roger Clemens pitched 7 1/3 innings at Yankee Stadium and was able to hold on to a 4-2 lead and earn the win. The next day Mike Hampton led the Mets to a win in the series finale. The entire City wanted more.

The excitement of the regular-season Subway Series was magnified exponentially in October. In the playoffs, the Yankees and Mets battled their way through San Francisco, Oakland, St. Louis and Seattle to bring the spotlight of the sports world onto our City for the first real Subway Series in 44 years. Wait till next year. …

The pictures within this book capture the triumph and adversity of a historic season. For fans of the Yankees and Mets, this book will bring back memories of the exhilaration and intensity that united—and divided—our City throughout the season and during a glorious October. For baseball fans everywhere, this book recalls the glory of the Subway Series era. It was a time when New York City was the undisputed Capital of Baseball. It is an era reborn through the 2000 season, a season that captured the imagination of a whole new generation of baseball fans.

Mayor Giuliani, here with Yankees owner George Steinbrenner, continues to cheer for the team he grew up cheering for.

an amazin' year

I t's one of the oldest adages in baseball – good pitching stops good hitting. That was never more evident than with the New York Mets of 2000.

The Mets, on surface level, were the same team as they were in 1999. They did not win enough games in the regular season to beat the Atlanta Braves or win the National League East title, but yet reached the playoffs as the wild card entry for the second consecutive year for the first time in franchise history.

There was a difference, however, and it was the improvement in the team's starting pitching that carried the Mets into the postseason and led them to their first World Championship since 1986.

"Every team strives for consistency," said first baseman Todd Zeile. "Having good starting pitching is the easiest way to become consistent. The teams that have it are the ones that usually don't hit the long, bad lows."

Make no mistake, the Mets had it in 2000. Led by lefthanders Mike Hampton and Al Leiter, all five regular starters won at least 11 games. Leiter won 16 and Hampton 15 and they finished fifth (Hampton) and sixth (Leiter) in the league in ERA. The third starter, Rick

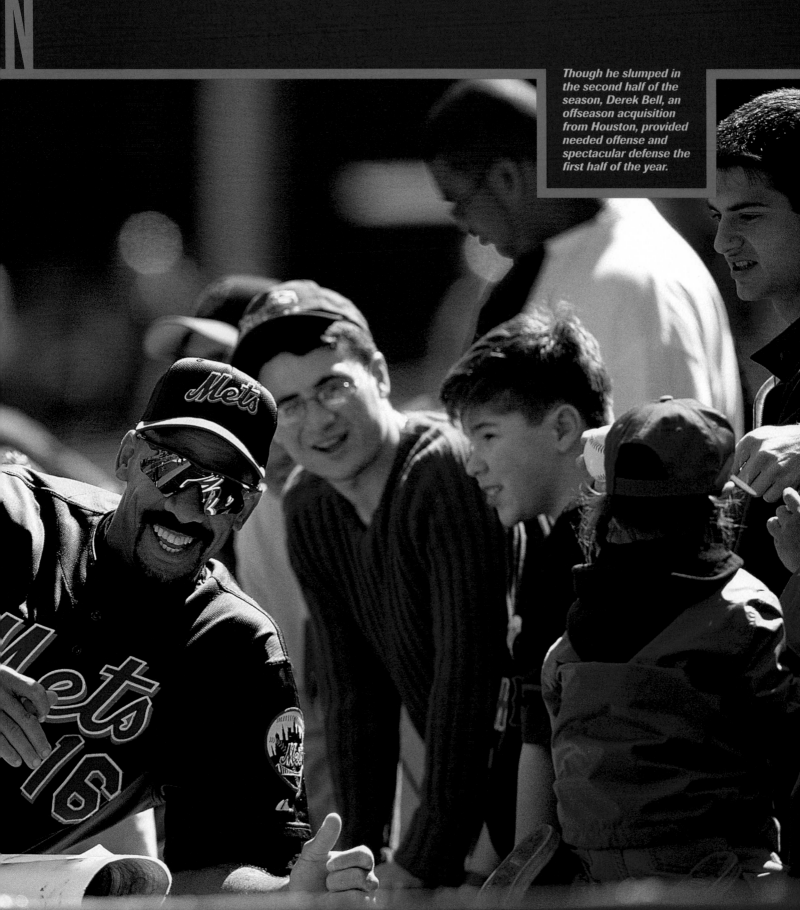

Though he slumped in the second half of the season, Derek Bell, an offseason acquisition from Houston, provided needed offense and spectacular defense the first half of the year.

Reed, was one of three other starters who each won 11 games. The biggest difference from the previous year came in the wins posted by those other two, the fourth and fifth starters, Glendon Rusch and Bobby J. Jones.

"Since I've been here, there always has been a chance you could get a well-pitched game out of one of our starters on a given day," said catcher Mike Piazza. "But it's a better chance now, and it's every day. You almost expect it now … I'm not comparing us with anyone. But generally, good teams have that."

The addition of Hampton, acquired in an offseason trade with Houston, gave the team its ace it had been lacking. The fact that he and Leiter both were lefthanded only made opponents' tasks that much more difficult, especially those loaded with lefthanded hitters.

"He's a fierce competitor and he has a lot of confidence in his ability," Zeile said. "And besides those two things, he's got the ability to go with it. There are a lot of guys who have the first two but not the last. It doesn't surprise me at all that he's tough and resilient."

The Mets starters, as a group, usually got games off to a good start. They allowed just 73 runs in the first inning, the fewest total in the National League. Their performances took pressure off the team's offense, and the deep, talented bullpen, led by closer Armando Benitez's career-high 41 saves, usually took care of the rest. The balance of lefthanders John Franco and Dennis Cook and righthanders Turk Wendell and Rick White gave manager Bobby Valentine a great deal of maneuverability.

For the first five months of the

He was tied for third in NL saves, with 41, but no one was more intimidating in the role of closer than Armando Benitez.

season, the offense was led by the MVP-level performance of Piazza, who was among the league leaders in homers, RBI and batting average. A late season slump – he hit only .231 in September – probably derailed his award chances, but didn't take away what he meant to the success of the team for the entire season.

It was impossible to discount his 38 homers, 113 RBI and .324 average that made him once again one of the most feared righthanded hitters in the game. It was his fifth consecutive season with 100 or more RBI.

"Anything I can do to help this team win is the most important thing," Piazza said. "Obviously, I am expected to hit. But my duties are a little bit more extensive as well behind the plate. If I can go out, catch a ballgame and we win the ballgame, that is what I'm supposed to do."

The improved starting pitching allowed the Mets the confidence they needed because of changes in their offensive and defensive performances. The team scored 40 percent of its runs on home runs, an inordinately high number, and the infield defense which might have been the best ever in 1999 was not as good this season. First baseman John Olerud left as a free agent and shortstop Rey Ordonez was felled by injury, but the play of Edgardo Alfonzo, one of the most underrated players in the game, and Robin Ventura, despite his offensive struggles, still was better than most.

The Mets also got a better-than-expected performance from rookie center fielder Jay Payton, whose 17 homers were the most by a Mets rookie since Darryl Strawberry hit 26 in 1983 and made him a solid candidate for

All Mike Piazza did was just about everything, leading the Mets in average (.324), home runs (38) and RBI (113).

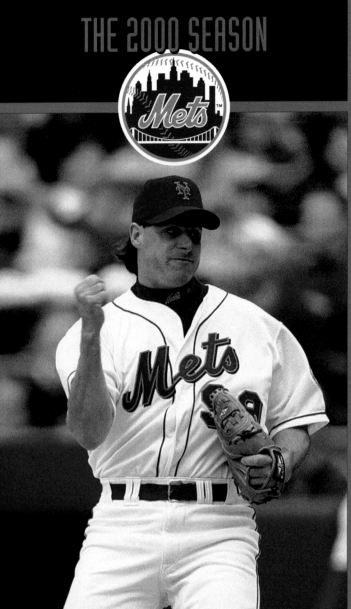

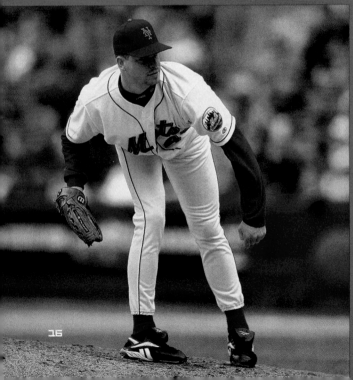

A staff that included, clockwise from left, Turk Wendell, Rick Reed, Mike Hampton, Dennis Cook, John Franco, Al Leiter, Bobby J. Jones and Glendon Rusch posted telling numbers: Tied for first in lowest on-base average, third in fewest walks allowed and third in strikeouts, third in runs allowed and tied for third in team ERA.

THE 2000 SEASON

Todd Zeile (below) signed on as a free agent acquisition and replaced John Olerud at first. As for Edgardo Alfonzo (bottom left): "When we're in a situation where we need a big hit and someone has to come through," says Darryl Hamilton, "everybody wants Fonzie at the plate."

Rookie of the Year.

For once, the Mets didn't have to worry about the Braves. In 1998, they were eliminated by the Braves on the final day of the regular season. In 1999, they won the wild card, upset Arizona in the division series, then lost the National League Championship Series to the Braves in six games.

Those teams didn't have the edge that the 2000 Mets possessed.

"Starting pitching can cover up a lot of shortcomings," said reliever Dennis Cook. "It's the one thing that usually can. If you're going to have a strength or an advantage, it's the one to have."

Playing in New York, it also doesn't hurt to have a tough skin. Together, as a team, the Mets were able to battle through the extra attention and distractions and get to the Series with the hope of becoming the second wild-card entry to win the Classic.

"This is a tough place to play," Zeile said. "It's like playing 162 World Series games during the regular season. To survive in this city is not easy. I think that's why this team is a lot like a family. There are a lot of good guys on this team, character guys. I know it's an overused term, but this team has the best chemistry of any team I've ever played on."

The Mets' offense was anchored, in part by Benny Agbayani (below, left) with a .289 average and 15 home runs and Jay Payton (above), .291 and 17 home runs. But contributions came from Joe McEwing (below, right) who hit just .222 but played five different positions, Todd Pratt (above, center) who hit .275 and Mike Bordick (above, right), a midseason acquisition who hit the first pitch he saw as a Met for a home run.

Much was made of Mike Piazza's supposed defensive weakness, but say this: Piazza guided one of the best pitching staffs in baseball, and he committed just three errors all season.

Manager Bobby Valentine had a number of new faces to plug into the lineup this year. Lenny Harris (above, from left) came from Arizona on June 2, Derek Bell came in a trade with Houston and Timo Perez was brought up from the minors on August 30. Outfielder Darryl Hamilton, acquired from Colorado in July of 1999, had his first full-season as a Met. Even with all of the new faces, Bobby V knew he could count on some old guard as well, such as Robin Ventura (below, left) and Edgardo Alfonzo.

Al Leiter led the team in strikeouts (200) and victories (16). Super-sub Joe McEwing, traded to the Mets from St. Louis in spring training, played five different positions during the season. Their approach to the game and their intensity provided fire to the team throughout the season.

BACK FOR MORE

For the first time in their dynasty, some cracks started to appear in the New York Yankees armor in 2000. There were questions, heretofore unnecessary, about the age of many of the team's key players. There were worries about the starting pitching. When they fell into a slump, which also was a new experience, there were concerns about whether the team could come out of it.

All of which makes their run for a third consecutive World Championship, hoping to become the first team to pull off the three-peat since the Oakland A's from 1972 to 1974, that much more spectacular.

"It was probably because of all this club went through all year," said manager Joe Torre. "So many questions about this club, would they be able to turn it on and off, all of that. I was just very proud of how they fought back, through the fatigue and everything else."

In previous years, the majority of the Yankees' problems concerned off-the-field activities. This year, the worries were on the field.

Age was beginning to show. Paul O'Neill was 37. David Cone was 4-14

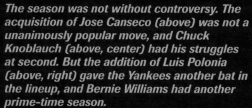

with a 6.91 ERA, pitching like a 37-year-old and not like a vintage David Cone. Roger Clemens was no longer a feared rival at age 38. Those weren't such big questions in July, and luckily for the Yankees, the rest of the American League East did not present a formidable challenge.

In September, however, the questions increased as talk of the postseason began. It didn't help public opinion that the Yankees lost their last seven games in the regular season, their longest slump of the season, and won only three of their last 18 games.

Was this the end of their fabulous run? Despite having still prime-time talented players in Derek Jeter, Bernie Williams and Mariano Rivera, was there enough left for another World Championship?

The longest previous Yankee losing streak going into the postseason was three games, in 1953.

Still, the Yankees did their best to convince themselves the first goal of any season had been accomplished. They had won their division, what they had set out to do when spring training had begun in February. How, and by how big a margin, didn't really matter.

How big a roller-coaster they had ridden between April and September didn't matter. They still had arrived at the end of the ride first. The fact they had a nine-game lead in the division on Sept. 13 before going on their biggest dive was only important to the statisticians.

It didn't matter that their final record of 87-74 was the worst of the eight teams that made the playoffs, and was three wins fewer than the Cleveland

The season was not without controversy. The acquisition of Jose Canseco (above) was not a unanimously popular move, and Chuck Knoblauch (above, center) had his struggles at second. But the addition of Luis Polonia (above, right) gave the Yankees another bat in the lineup, and Bernie Williams had another prime-time season.

For three Yankees stalwarts, their numbers tell the story. Paul O'Neill (left, above) hit .283, with 18 home runs and 100 RBI. Catcher Jorge Posada (left, below) hit .287, with 28 home runs and 86 RBI. And Mariano Rivera had a 2.85 ERA and saved 36 of 41 opportunities.

Indians had recorded, and the Indians were staying home in October. It didn't matter they won only one more game than the Dodgers, who fired their manager.

By Yankees standards, this was an ordinary year. The Yankees ranked in the middle of the American League pack in almost every statistical category. The pitching was not as dominant as it had been in years past, raising the stress level of the position players. When they didn't hit as well as in years past, it put more pressure on the pitchers. That was not the combination this team and its fans were used to watching.

Jeter hit .339, but didn't have as dominating a season as he has enjoyed in the Yankees' past championship runs. Tino Martinez hit .258, his lowest average as a Yankee. Chuck Knoblauch struggled offensively as well as defensively and lost his place in the starting lineup to Luis Sojo, acquired in August from Pittsburgh. Scott Brosius hit just .230. O'Neill did not have an extra-base hit after Sept. 6.

But then there were extraordinary individual seasons as well.

Williams had a career-high 31 homers and 121 RBI. It was his fourth season of driving in more than 100 runs and also scoring 100 or more. The only other Yankees to do that three times in their careers were Babe Ruth, Lou Gehrig and Joe DiMaggio.

Catcher Jorge Posada set career highs in every offensive category. New addition David Justice hit 20 homers after joining the team in a trade from Cleveland at the end of June. Andy Pettitte led the staff with 19 wins.

"We've spoiled people," said third base coach Willie Randolph. "People sit

at home and get tired of seeing us pour champagne. We are the team everyone wants to beat. I don't think people realize how difficult it is to stay where we are."

In the end, what mattered most was something the players didn't lose during the season – their pride and their confidence. That intangible combination proved to all of their September skeptics that their worries had been a waste of time.

It also proved to Torre that there was a big difference between predicting the team's death and actually watching it happen.

"Don't believe everything you read in the papers," Torre said. "If you happen to see your name in the obituary column, I wouldn't lay down if I were you."

When it counted most, the Yankees were not lying down.

"We have proven year after year that we will find a way to win," said general manager Brian Cashman. "You always wonder if you can sustain the motivation. You climb the mountain, and then there is another mountain. Can you keep climbing? I will always believe these players will keep climbing."

Twice a rival—as a Brave and as an Indian—David Justice came to the Yanks in June and promptly led the team in home runs (41) and was second in RBI, with 118.

With Tino Martinez (below, left), Jose Vizcaino (below, top), Scott Brosius (below, bottom) and Derek Jeter, the Yankees' infield was solid, if not spectacular, most of the time.

Manager Joe Torre and coach Don Zimmer got power from the midseason acquisition of Glenallen Hill (left) with 27 home runs, and Paul O'Neill (below), with 18; they got defense from catcher Jorge Posada, who threw out almost a third of the runners who tried to steal on the Yanks.

Yankees pitching allowed the fourth-fewest runs in the league and the third-lowest on-base average. While Roger Clemens (above, left) and Andy Pettitte (above, right) dominated at times, there were key contributions from David Cone, Mike Stanton, Dwight Gooden, Jeff Nelson, Denny Neagle and Randy Choate.

While Torre had some versatile parts to plug into his lineup and spell regulars—like (lower left) Luis Sojo, who came from Pittsburgh, Chris Turner (upper right) and Clay Bellinger (below)—he also knew he could count on his veterans—El Duque, Orlando Hernandez (left), and Andy Pettitte (right).

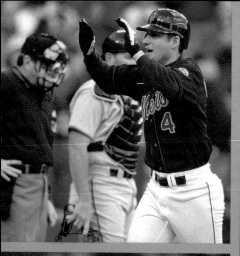

THE SECOND SEASON

Giants   **5**
Mets   **1**

Game 1: October 4
Pac Bell Park

It was a one-inning nightmare, the kind that can disrupt best-laid plans and illusions of grandeur. When Mets lefthander Mike Hampton retired the first two Giants in the third inning of a 1-1 Division Series battle, he did not imagine that the beautiful blue San Francisco sky was about to fall on his head.

Bill Mueller triggered the collapse with a single to left-center field and Barry Bonds followed with a tie-breaking triple that eluded right fielder Derek Bell, who sprained an ankle while chasing the ball. Hampton was forced to wait about five minutes while the Mets tended to Bell. When action resumed, Hampton walked Jeff Kent before delivering a pitch that Ellis Burks slammed off the left field foul pole for a three-run homer.

"I should have had Mike throw more warmups when I was out in right field," Mets manager Bobby Valentine said. "He lost his rhythm after Derek got hurt and he threw one down the middle to Ellis, who did what he should do to it."

On a gloriously sunny San Francisco afternoon, the Giants' Livan Hernandez outdueled Mike Hampton. Ellis Burks broke open a tight game with a three-run homer and the Mets never got anything going on offense.

Mets 5
Giants 4

Game 2: October 5
Pac Bell Park

The ball sailed majestically toward the right field stands, a season-threatening arrow aimed expertly at the heart of the frantic Mets. When pinch hitter J.T. Snow's ninth-inning shot rattled high off the right field facing for a game-tying three-run homer, revved-up Giants fans delivered a roaring eulogy.

Gone in that memorable instant was a seemingly safe 4-1 Mets lead, the sterling effort of starter Al Leiter, the confidence of closer Armando Benitez and a chance to square the series. Gone, too, was the Mets' hard-earned momentum—but not their hope.

"We knew we were going to get another chance to go up there and swing the bats," said center fielder Jay Payton. "Fortunately, it worked out for us."

Down but not out, the Mets fought back in the 10th. Payton came through with a run-scoring single, and when John Franco retired the Giants in the bottom of the inning, the Mets headed home with an emotional victory.

SERIES 2000

After Edgardo Alfonzo's homer had given the Mets the lead in the ninth, the Giants celebrated J.T. Snow's ninth-inning pinch-hit blast that tied the game. Then, an inning later, after Jay Payton's single had given the Mets the lead again, John Franco shut the door and the Mets left San Francisco tied, 1-1, in the series.

Mets 3
Giants 2

Game 3: October 7
Shea Stadium

t took 5 hours, 22 minutes and 13 grueling innings, but the gain far exceeded the pain as the Mets inched toward their first NLCS appearance since 1988. Relief was provided by a stingy bullpen and stocky left fielder Benny Agbayani, who delivered a dramatic one-out solo home run off Aaron Fultz to end the Shea Stadium marathon.

"It's a great feeling to be the man," Agbayani said after getting his only hit in six at-bats. "We're one of those teams that never say die. We know anything can happen."

For most of the night, very little happened offensively. The Giants scored two fourth-inning runs off starter Rick Reed. The Mets scored one in the sixth and tied the game in the eighth on Edgardo Alfonzo's two-out double off fireballing closer Robb Nen, who had saved 28 straight games. The Giants failed to score over the final nine innings against Reed and five Mets relievers, who allowed only four hits with Rick White picking up the win.

Benny Agbayani ended Game 3 in dramatic fashion—a walk-off home run in the 13th inning.

Mets 4
Giants 0

Game 4: October 8
Shea Stadium

The fireworks exploded high above the left field fence, just as the Mets exploded from their dugout to mob Bobby J. Jones. The long-awaited return of New York to the NLCS spotlight was enough to send Shea into a frenzy, but the method to the madness of 56,245 delirious fans was an unexpected bonus.

Jones, who got the start only after much deliberation by manager Bobby Valentine, was almost perfect while throwing the sixth complete-game one-hitter in postseason history, allowing only a fifth-inning double by Jeff Kent. Jones' slow, slower and slowest deliveries kept the Giants' big bats off balance and he retired the final 13 batters he faced. The only serious Giants threat came in the fifth, when Jones got pitcher Mark Gardner on a bases-loaded popup.

"Just textbook pitching. He really knew how to work the hitters," catcher Mike Piazza said. "As the game wore on, he just got tougher and tougher."

Bobby J. Jones allowed only one hit in a complete-game performance, and the Mets got big hits from Robin Ventura (above), who had a two-run homer, and Edgardo Alfonzo, who had a two-run double, as the Mets rolled into the NLCS.

A's   5
Yankees   3

October 3
Network Associates Coliseum

The sounds shot through the crisp Oakland air, creating unsettling vibrations that could be felt a continent away in New York. For the young, free-spirited and fearless Oakland A's, the screaming mayhem of 47,360 Bay Area fans played like an inspirational baseball symphony.

"The only time we get that (from fans) is when we play San Francisco in interleague games," marveled catcher Ramon Hernandez after the A's had pounced on the two-time defending World Series-champion Yankees in Game 1 of the Division Series at Network Associates Coliseum. And, of course, when they go out to slay a monster.

Hernandez drove in two runs and combined with Eric Chavez and Jeremy Giambi—the bottom third of Oakland's order—for six hits and four runs scored as the A's wiped out an early 2-0 Yankees lead, defeating Roger Clemens and driving home an important point for the defending champions.

The moment of truth comes early in a five-game series.

Ramon Hernandez's hit in the sixth gave the A's the lead, but the Yankees kept it close by cutting down Jeremy Giambi at the plate.

Yankees 4
A's 0

October 4
Network Associates Coliseum

Andy Pettitte played the straight man. Glenallen Hill and Luis Sojo delivered the punch line. When all was said and done on a brisk fall evening in the Oakland Bay Area, the joke was on all those baseball fans who had delivered premature eulogies on the latest Yankees dynasty.

"This was a huge game for us," said Pettitte, who shut down the hot-hitting A's on five hits over 7 2/3 innings. Pettitte's wakeup call came just in time. After sleepwalking with the Yankees through a season-ending seven-game losing streak and a loss in the Division Series opener, the veteran lefthander threw a sweeping curve at 47,860 emotional Oakland fans.

A's righthander Kevin Appier matched Pettitte pitch for pitch through five innings, but the Yankees took control in the sixth when designated hitter Hill, with runners at first and second, delivered a two-out, run-scoring single. Sojo followed with a two-run, opposite-field double that gave Pettitte and closer Mariano Rivera all the cushion they needed.

SERIES 2000

It was all Andy Pettitte in Game 2, 7 2/3 scoreless innings that evened the series as it went back to New York.

GAME ③ A.L. DIVISIO

Yankees 4
A's 2

October 6
Yankee Stadium

He fidgeted and tugged nervously at his cap and jersey. Every pitch was delivered with uncomfortable determination. Orlando Hernandez might not have been his usual artistic self on this special October night at Yankee Stadium, but the result was another playoff masterpiece.

"For the first five innings, my control was terrible and my team was encouraging me," El Duque told reporters through a translator. "After the fifth inning, Mr. (Joe) Torre pulled me aside and said stop battling yourself and pitch your game."

The Cuban righthander, who had entered the 2000 playoffs with a 5-0 postseason record and 1.02 ERA, battled through seven innings, allowing only four hits while walking five and throwing 130 pitches.

But all the A's could muster out of his struggle were single runs in the second and fifth innings—and nothing over the final two off closer Mariano Rivera.

SERIES 2000

Bernie Williams scored one of the Yankees' four runs, Luis Sojo and the Yankees' infield turned two double plays, and El Duque raised his postseason record to 6-0 in the Yankees' Game 3 victory.

A's 11
Yankees 1

October 7
Yankee Stadium

One was a well-decorated veteran, a five-time Cy Young winner with a battle-tested right arm. The other was a 22-year-old rookie making his postseason debut in a must-win situation. But a funny thing happened to Roger Clemens on the Yankees' way to a fifth ALCS appearance in five years.

Oakland lefthander Barry Zito shrugged off the pressure and outpitched The Rocket before 56,915 fans at Yankee Stadium. Zito scattered seven hits over 5 2/3 innings while another unlikely hero, Olmedo Saenz, set the table with a stunning three-run, first-inning home run. Not only did Saenz deliver an early message that the brash A's were not ready to give in to the Yankees mystique, he put a quick damper on the festive atmosphere that might have intimidated some opponents.

"Shoot, we won the division on the last day of the season, we are going to a fifth game; they make movies about this stuff," said A's first baseman Jason Giambi, who scored a pair of runs. "We are in the middle of a 'Rocky' movie right now."

Eric Chavez had two hits and two RBI and scored two runs as the A's routed Roger Clemens, forcing a decisive Game 5 in Oakland.

Yankees 7
A's 5

October 8
Network Associates Coliseum

Too old. Too slow. Uninspired. Inconsistent offense. Unreliable bullpen. When push came to shove and a season was on the line for the most celebrated franchise in baseball, the Oakland A's and 41,170 hungry fans watched the Bronx Bombers defy their harshest critics while swallowing a huge dose of Yankee mystique.

Oakland's reality check came in a shocking first inning when the Yankees jumped on starter Gil Heredia for six runs, three coming on a towering double by Tino Martinez that was misjudged by center fielder Terrence Long. Chuck Knoblauch, who returned to his leadoff spot after being benched for three games, singled twice, scored a run and drove in another during the early explosion.

Although in control the entire game, the victory was not easy. Game 2 winner Andy Pettitte couldn't stand prosperity and allowed five runs before giving way to the bullpen with two out in the fourth. Mike Stanton, Jeff Nelson, Orlando Hernandez and Mariano Rivera slammed the door on the A's, allowing only three more hits.

SERIES 2000

After a long overnight flight to the West Coast, the Yankees started early in Game 5. Tino Martinez's first-inning double scored Derek Jeter, Paul O'Neill and David Justice. The early 6-0 lead held up, and the Yankees were headed to the ALCS.

Mets 8
Cardinals 2

October 11
Busch Memorial Stadium

Ignoring the deafening roar of 52,255 fans and defying critics of his postseason history, Mets lefthander Mike Hampton parted the red sea at Busch Stadium with seven innings of six-hit ball that gave the wild-card Mets a welcome jump in the opener of the National League Championship Series.

"I just wanted to do my part to help this team win," said Hampton, who carried an 0-2 playoff record and 5.87 ERA into the game. "I didn't do that in the first series (against the Giants). I wanted to focus and concentrate on being a contributor instead of a liability—and really go out and prove something."

Hampton's teammates provided a quick lift, jumping on Cardinals starter Darryl Kile for two first-inning runs—one on a Mike Piazza double and another on Robin Ventura's sacrifice fly—and Hampton carried a 3-0 advantage into the seventh when the Cardinals put runners on first and second with one out. Edgar Renteria's drive into the right

SHIP SERIES 2000

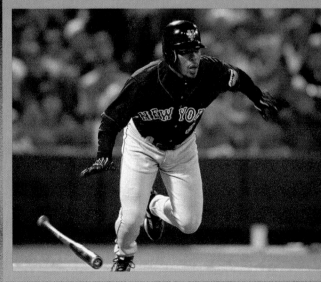

field corner was tracked down on a nice catch by Timo Perez and Jim Edmonds brought the crowd to its feet when he drove left fielder Benny Agbayani to the left-center field wall.

"I didn't breathe, I'll tell you that," Hampton said, referring to Edmonds' drive. "I was going to breathe, but I thought I might push the ball over the fence."

The only St. Louis runs, both unearned, came off Armando Benitez in the ninth, after the Mets had scored three times in the top of the inning.

While Mike Hampton shut down the vaunted Cardinals offense, led by Jim Edmonds, Edgardo Alfonzo (above) and the Mets teed off on Cardinals pitching, including ninth-inning home runs by Todd Zeile (far left) and Jay Payton (below) off reliever Mike James.

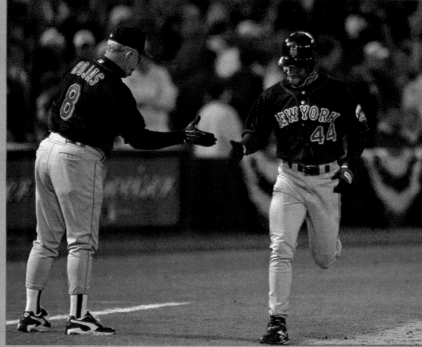

Mets: 6
Cardinals: 5

October 12
Busch Memorial Stadium

Much of the post–Game 2 discussion focused on the wildness of Cardinals rookie lefthander Rick Ankiel, but in the end it was the late-inning heroics of Mets center fielder Jay Payton that made the difference—again.

Payton, who decided Game 2 of the Division Series against the Giants with a 10th-inning single, broke a 5-5 tie against St. Louis with a critical ninth-inning single, ending the Cardinals' comeback hopes. The Mets had led 2-0, 3-1 and 5-3, but each time the Cardinals fought back to tie. The game-winner was set up by first baseman Will Clark's error on a Robin Ventura grounder.

"It's amazing, but we keep coming back," said Mets starter Al Leiter. "That's kind of been the way we're playing, very resilient."

The Mets benefited early from Ankiel's wildness. Ankiel, who had self-destructed a week earlier in a Division Series game against Atlanta, walked three batters, fired two wild pitches and

It began with unprecedented wildness from Cardinals starter Rick Ankiel, and ended with Joe McEwing, a pinch-runner for Robin Ventura, scoring the winning run in the ninth. In between, it was Al Leiter once again shutting down the Cardinals' offense.

While John Franco, Turk Wendell and Armando Benitez frustrated the Cardinals, the offense was supplied by Mike Piazza, who was 1-for-2 with three walks, and Edgardo Alfonzo, who was 2-for-3 with two walks.

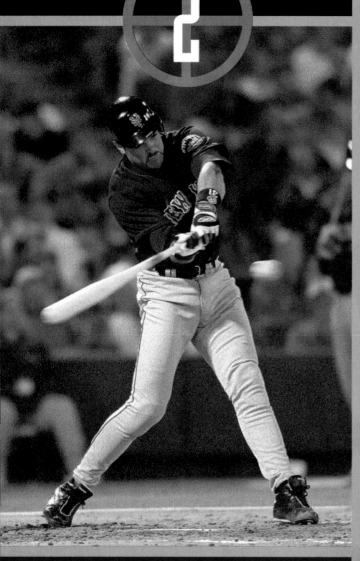

gave up two first-inning runs before being relieved by Britt Reames. Mike Piazza's third-inning home run and eighth-inning RBI singles by Edgardo Alfonzo and Todd Zeile set the stage for Payton.

"To get out of (St. Louis) up 2-0 and going back to our place is a good feeling," Leiter said.

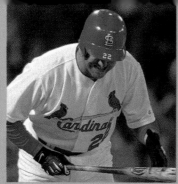

Southwestern Bell

Not only did Cardinals hitting go dormant, it's defense did too. The Mets got the offense when it counted, from Benny Agbayani, among others; and the defense as well, such as this sliding catch by Timo Perez.

Cardinals 8
Mets 2

October 14
Shea Stadium

The 55,693 roaring, towel-waving fans at Shea Stadium were primed for a celebration amid rumblings of a Subway Series. The Mets, already up two games, were primed for the kill. The opposing pitcher, plagued by a sore knee, would be making his first start in 13 days. All, it seemed, was right in New York.

But the Cardinals, unwilling to roll over and play dead, changed that perception in Game 3, thanks to the surprising effort of righthander Andy Benes and the timely hitting that had deserted them in the first two games at St. Louis. Benes worked eight strong innings, allowed two runs on six hits.

"You can't measure the heart of the guys in this dugout over here," Benes said. "Our guys have fought all year, and you know it's going to be a really great series."

The Cardinals, susceptible to Mets lefthanders, broke on top when Jim Edmonds doubled home two first-inning runs off righthander Rick Reed. After the Mets scored once in the bottom of the inning, the Cardinals added two in the

The Cardinals got to Rick Reed early and often in Game 3, as the Cardinals pulled back a game as the series came to Queens.

third, one in the fourth and three in the fifth, going 7-for-16 with runners in scoring position.

The most excitement for the New York crowd came in the fourth, when Mark McGwire, reduced to pinch-hitting duty because of a sore knee, flied moderately deep to left with the bases loaded.

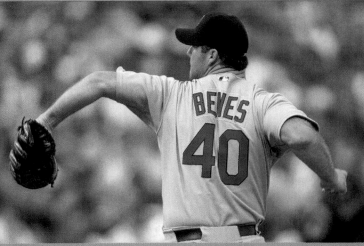

Will Clark was gunned down at the plate, but that was one of the few bright spots for the Mets in Game 3. Behind Andy Benes' pitching, and the offense of Edgar Renteria, J.D. Drew and Clark, the Cardinals easily took Game 3.

Mets 10
Cardinals 6

October 15
Shea Stadium

The Cardinals struck first. But the Mets struck harder and longer. And the result was a big New York victory that put the Mets within one game of their first World Series since 1986.

The 55,665 fans at Shea Stadium were shocked into silence for the second straight day when Cardinals center fielder Jim Edmonds connected for a two-run homer off Bobby J. Jones in the opening inning—the fourth consecutive game in which the opposing team had scored twice in the first. But the Mets struck back with a vengeance, scoring four first-inning runs on an LCS-record five doubles by Timo Perez, Edgardo Alfonzo, Mike Piazza, Robin Ventura and Benny Agbayani. Todd Zeile's two-run double and Agbayani's RBI single scored three more in the second off Cardinals ace Darryl Kile.

"We had good success getting to him early," Zeile said. "It seemed like the balls he got hurt on were fastballs in counts that he had to come in on."

The Cardinals continued to plug away

SHIP SERIES 2000

The Mets struck early on Cardinals ace Darryl Kile, with a record five doubles in the first inning. Timo Perez led it off with a double, then came doubles by Edgardo Alfonzo, Mike Piazza, Robin Ventura (not pictured) and Benny Agbayani.

After the Mets struck in the first to catch the Cardinals after Jim Edmonds' home run, Mets fans began to sense a Subway Series. The Cardinals' defense crumbled—Fernando Tatis booted a ball—their frustration began to show—Dave Duncan argued a call—then John Franco and Armando Benitez closed out another victory.

against Jones and pulled to within 8-6 after five innings, but Glendon Rusch, John Franco and Armando Benitez slammed the door and gave the Mets an opportunity to close out the series in New York.

"We're 27 good outs away from being in the World Series," said Rusch, who worked three scoreless innings for the win.

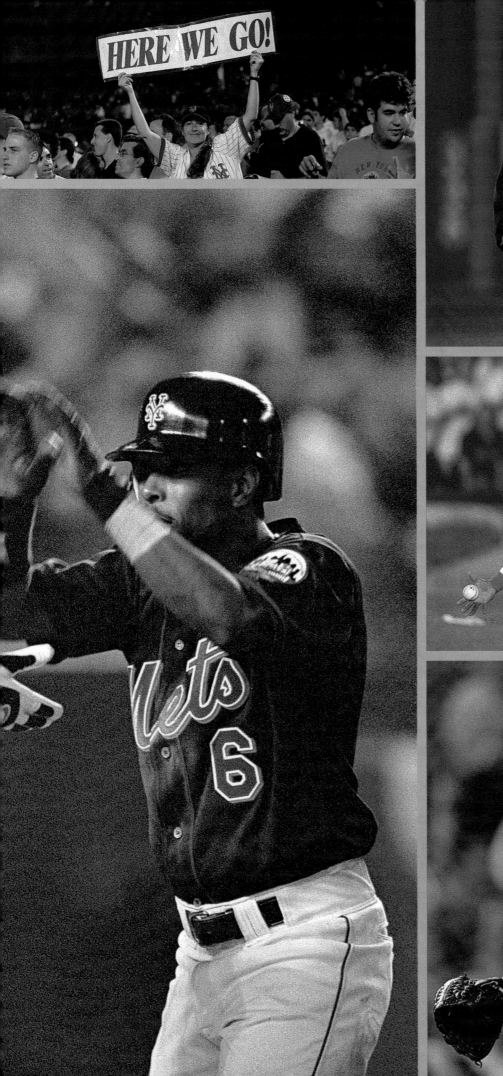

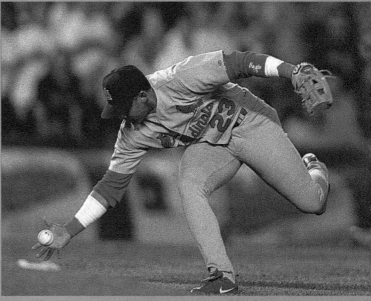

Mets 7
Cardinals 0

October 16
Shea Stadium

It started in the first inning when the Mets scored three times against the reeling Cardinals. It ended hours later, in the wee hours of the brisk New York morning, when the last champagne was sprayed. Game 5 of the N.L. Championship Series was one big party for a city that knows how to celebrate.

The three-run first, supplemented by Todd Zeile's three-run fourth-inning double off Cardinals starter Pat Hentgen, was more than enough offense for lefthander Mike Hampton, who went all the way on a sparkling three-hit shutout. The victory gave the Mets their first pennant since 1986. It also kept alive New Yorkers' hopes for the first Subway Series since 1956.

"I'm rooting for the Yankees (in the ALCS) to be perfectly honest," Zeile said. "I'd love to see a Subway Series. We have some unfinished business with the Yankees."

When the final out was recorded, the Mets ran a victory lap around Shea Stadium before heading for the

The Mets battered Cardinals starter Pat Hentgen with a number of big hits in Game 5.

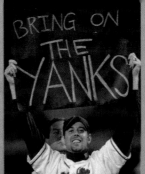

clubhouse. The celebration later returned to the field where backup catcher Todd Pratt sprayed delighted fans with champagne.

Inside or out, most of the credit was given to Hampton, who dominated the Cardinals. "He pitched the game of his life," manager Bobby Valentine said. "And mine."

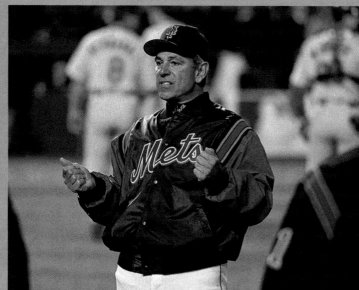

With pitching, defense, hitting and intensity, the Mets matched the Cardinals on everything in the series. When it was done, John Franco, Bobby Valentine and the rest of the Mets celebrated, knowing they had done their part in ensuring a Subway Series.

Mariners 2
Yankees 0

October 10
Yankee Stadium

The message, delivered emphatically by the young Seattle Mariners, came through loud and clear. They would not be awed by the Yankee mystique, intimidated by 54,481 snarling New York fans or mesmerized by the championship aura of the greatest franchise in baseball history.

The Yanks stumbled out of the gate in the ALCS, thanks to the pitching of Mariners starter Freddy Garcia.

ALCS
1

Rickey Henderson (above) was back in the Bronx, and his single scored Mark McLemore (below) with the game's first run. Then a procession of Mariners pitchers, with Kazuhiro Sasaki (right) closing, kept Derek Jeter, Luis Sojo and the rest of the Yankees batters off-balance all night. The bat of Alex Rodriguez (bottom right) supplied an insurance-run homer.

Their victory in the A.L. Championship Series opener at Yankee Stadium was shockingly efficient.

"If they pitch like they pitched tonight, then we're not going to win the series," said Yankees reliever Jeff Nelson.

Freddy Garcia, a 24-year-old righthander, provided the biggest hurdle for the Yankees over 6 2/3 three-hit innings. But relievers Jose Paniagua, Arthur Rhodes and Kazuhiro Sasaki combined for three-hit relief with Sasaki picking up his third save of the playoffs. Garcia stranded Yankees at third base in the third and fifth innings and escaped a two-on-nobody-out jam in the sixth by striking out Paul O'Neill and Bernie Williams and getting David Justice on a deep fly ball.

The Yankees got a strong 5⅔ innings from lefthander Denny Neagle, but Rickey Henderson's run-scoring single in the fifth and a solo sixth-inning home run by Alex Rodriguez provided all the offense the Mariners needed.

"We have to attack them, attack them early and be ready to go to war," Rodriguez said. "They're going to come out real hungry and be ready to go to war tomorrow."

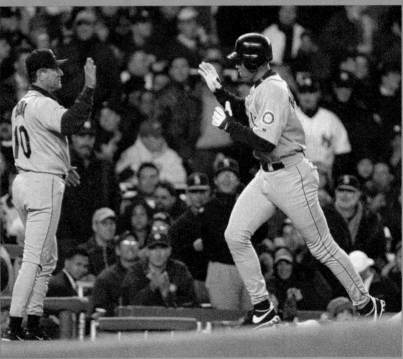

GAME 2 A.L. CHAMPI

Yankees 7
Mariners 1

October 11
Yankee Stadium

The brilliant New York sunshine was fading into dusk, as were Yankee hopes for a third straight World Series championship. But then a not-so-funny thing happened to the Seattle Mariners. The Bronx Bombers, mired in a 21-inning scoreless streak, exploded for seven eighth-inning runs and transformed frustration into series-turning momentum.

"Down 2-0 going into Seattle would've been devastating," said second baseman Chuck Knoblauch, who contributed a run-scoring single to the uprising. "And right now, we're riding a high with the eighth inning."

The rally was sudden and devastating. John Halama had shut out the Yankees on five hits over the first six innings and Jose Paniagua had worked a scoreless seventh. When Arthur Rhodes took the mound with the Mariners leading 1-0 in the eighth, the Yankees had tied a franchise-record postseason scoreless streak and appeared helpless in scoring situations.

That would end. David Justice opened the inning with a double and the Yankees went on to collect an LCS-record eight hits, including a home run by Derek Jeter. The rally re-energized the 55,317 fans at Yankee Stadium—and removed a major burden from

John Halama had the Yanks blanked until the eighth. Down 1-0 in the game, and looking at the possibility of going down 2-0 in the series, the Yankees scored seven in the eighth, capped by Derek Jeter's home run off of Mariners reliever Jose Mesa.

ALCS
2

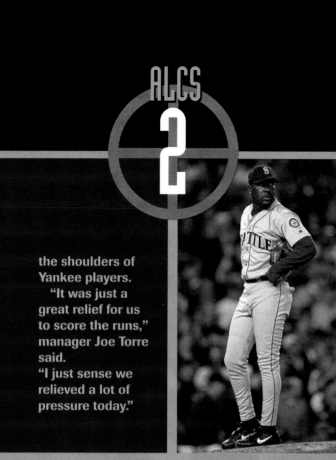

the shoulders of Yankee players.

"It was just a great relief for us to score the runs," manager Joe Torre said.

"I just sense we relieved a lot of pressure today."

Mariners reliever Arthur Rhodes (far left) took the brunt of the Yankees' eighth, an inning that started with a David Justice double and ended with a David Justice strikeout (below), but Rhodes was gone by the time Luis Sojo scored the Yanks' fourth run. El Duque was the star on the mound, holding the Mariners to one run, and Tino Martinez was the star at bat, going 3-for-4, including a single in the big eighth inning.

Yankees 8
Mariners 2

October 13
Safeco Field

Like a grumpy bear waking up after a long winter slumber, the Yankees tossed aside the Mariners in Game 3 and gave 47,827 screaming fans at Safeco Field a glimpse of their typical October magic.

Bernie Williams, Tino Martinez and David Justice provided most of the offensive sleight of hand while lefthander Andy Pettitte, far from top form, held the Mariners at bay for 6⅔ innings before turning matters over to Jeff Nelson and Mariano Rivera. From timely hitting to clutch pitching, everything appeared to be back in sync for the long-stumbling Yanks.

After spotting the Mariners a 1-0 lead in the first inning, the Yankees took a second-inning lead on back-to-back home runs by Williams and Martinez and gradually stretched their margin with a run in the sixth and four in the ninth—two on a single by Justice. When Rivera worked 1⅔ innings for the save, he stretched his postseason scoreless innings streak to 33⅓, breaking the long-standing record of Yankees lefthander Whitey Ford.

The Yankee victory was punctuated by an offense that generated 13 hits and scored in four different innings for the first time in the playoffs. Even slumping right fielder Paul O'Neill (0-for-8 in the series) got in on the act, driving in his first postseason run with a sixth-inning single.

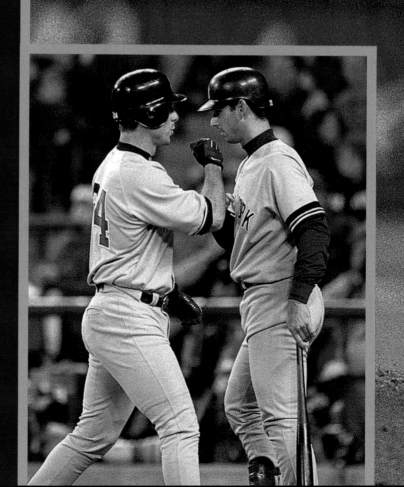

Tino Martinez's second-inning homer staked Andy Pettitte to a 2-1 lead in the game and, eventually, the Yankees to a 2-1 lead in the series.

Bernie Williams was 3-for-4, including this home run in Game 3 (above, left); Tino Martinez followed Williams with another solo homer, despite the best efforts of Mariners outfielder Mike Cameron; Paul O'Neill also drove home a run with a single (above, right). Meanwhile, Mariners shortstop Alex Rodriguez was busy, here on a play with Jose Vizcaino (right), and (below) in a first-inning meeting with his Yankees counterpart, Derek Jeter, on a double play.

Yankees   5
Mariners   0

October 14
Safeco Field

They call him The Rocket, a nickname Roger Clemens had lived up to many times over his sensational 17-year career. But never was it more appropriate than in Game 4 at Safeco Field, when the big righthander shot down the Mariners and blasted the Yankees into position to claim their fourth American League pennant in five years and 37th overall.

"It was total dominance," marveled manager Joe Torre after watching Clemens shut out Seattle on one hit—a seventh-inning double by Al Martin off the glove of leaping first baseman Tino Martinez.

"Tonight was special," said Clemens. "The ball was jumping out of my hand."

Clemens used his 97-mph fastball to strike out 15 Mariners, an ALCS nine-inning record. He walked two, including shortstop Alex Rodriguez in a contentious first inning in which Clemens brushed back the young slugger with two high-and-tight fastballs. Mariners starter Paul Abbott buzzed Yankees catcher Jorge Posada in the second, but nothing else developed.

While Clemens was overmatching hitters, Derek Jeter and David Justice were

Roger Clemens struck out 15 in Game 4, and walked just two, one of which was in a first-inning battle with Alex Rodriguez.

4

supplying the power—home runs that accounted for all the Yankee runs. Other than Martin's leadoff hit in the seventh, the Mariners never came close to scoring.

"It's really tough to beat this one for a postseason game," Torre said. "Don Larsen's postseason (perfect) game (in the 1956 World Series) was pretty damn good, but this was total dominance tonight."

The Mariners' Al Martin had the only hit off Roger Clemens, a seventh-inning double. Clemens faced just 30 batters, retiring 15 by strikeout, five on groundballs, seven on flyballs. The only offense the Yankees would need was supplied in the form of home runs by Derek Jeter and David Justice.

	1	2	3	4	5	6	7	8	9	R	H	E
NYY	0	0	0	0	3	0	0	2	0	5	5	0
SEA	0	0	0	0	0	0	0	0	0	0	1	0

Mariners 6
Yankees 2

October 15
Safeco Field

All they needed was a little push, a big shove and some good, old-fashioned desperation. With their backs planted firmly against the wall, the Mariners came alive to win Game 5 of the ALCS and at least temporarily derail the Yankees' World Series express.

Playing what might have been their final game in their first full season at Safeco Field, slumbering Seattle hitters awoke in a five-run fifth inning that spelled doom for Yankees lefthander Denny Neagle and provided all the support Freddy Garcia would need to record his second victory of the series and force a Game 6 in New York.

"We just want to get it to Game 7 and extend it, somehow, some way, and make it a little difficult on these New Yorkers," shortstop Alex Rodriguez said.

Rodriguez delivered a two-run, fifth-inning single off reliever Jeff Nelson, wiping out Neagle's 2-1 lead. Edgar Martinez followed with a two-run homer and John Olerud concluded the uprising with a solo shot. Garcia worked five innings for the Mariners

SHIP SERIES 2000

The M's stayed alive, getting to Yankees starter Denny Neagle. Alex Rodriguez drove in two runs, and Kaz Sasaki allowed no runs in his 1 2/3 innings.

Tino Martinez (below, left) was 1-for-4 in Game 5. The Mariners' Edgar Martinez (below, middle and right) was 1-for-3, his one hit this fifth-inning homer. Bernie Williams (bottom, left) took a home run away from John Olerud, but Olerud hit one later in the game. Jay Buhner (bottom, right) went 2-for-4 in the game.

and Jose Paniagua, Arthur Rhodes and Kazuhiro Sasaki finished up.

"One of those days," said Nelson. "Those are the main two guys (Rodriguez and Martinez) I want to face. Either I'm going to get 'em, or they're going to get me. I got 'em the other day, but today wasn't very good."

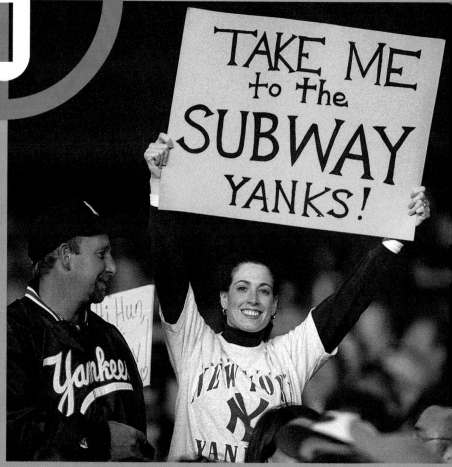

Yankees 9
Mariners 7

October 17
Yankee Stadium

I t was a shot in the dark, a rocket that carried the Yankees to their third straight A.L. pennant. David Justice's stunning three-run, seventh-inning blast off Seattle's Arthur Rhodes also was destiny, a memorable home run that set up the Yankees' first World Series meeting with the N.L.-champion Mets and the first Subway Series since 1956.

For the Mariners, who squandered an early

Riding David Justice's three-run home run in the seventh inning, the Yankees rallied from four runs down to set up the showdown in the Subway Series.

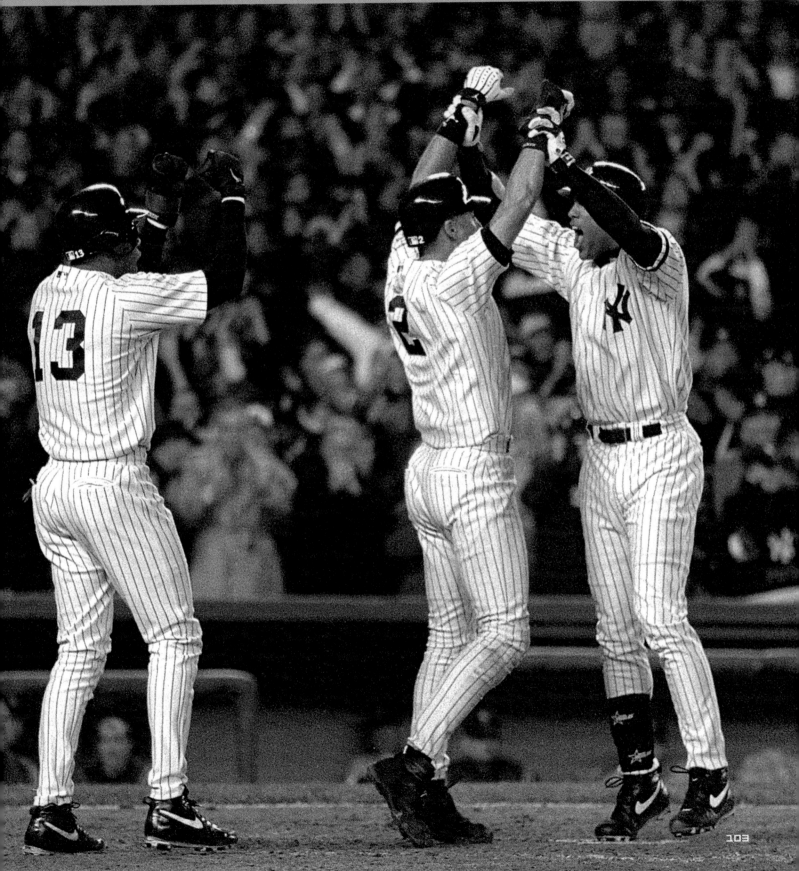

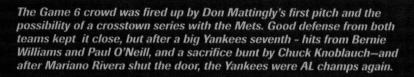
The Game 6 crowd was fired up by Don Mattingly's first pitch and the possibility of a crosstown series with the Mets. Good defense from both teams kept it close, but after a big Yankees seventh - hits from Bernie Williams and Paul O'Neill, and a sacrifice bunt by Chuck Knoblauch—and after Mariano Rivera shut the door, the Yankees were AL champs again.

4-0 lead, it was a bomb that ripped apart their championship dreams. Leading 4-3 with one out in the bottom of the seventh, Rhodes was brought in to face Justice with two men on base. Justice worked the count to 3-1 before delivering his game-deciding blast—one that sent 56,598 Yankee Stadium fans into a frenzy.

"It was magical," said Justice, who watched his teammates score three more times in the six-run inning. "It was unbelievable when I rounded the bases, to see this place erupt."

The home run made a winner of Orlando Hernandez, who became the first pitcher to record an 8-0 postseason record. El Duque worked seven chippy innings before giving way to Mariano Rivera, who finally closed the door on the Yankees' 37th pennant after the Mariners had scored three eighth-inning runs.

"This city is going to be crazy," predicted shortstop Derek Jeter.

"I have a feeling the city is not going to be the same for the next 10 days, and maybe after that," added manager Joe Torre.

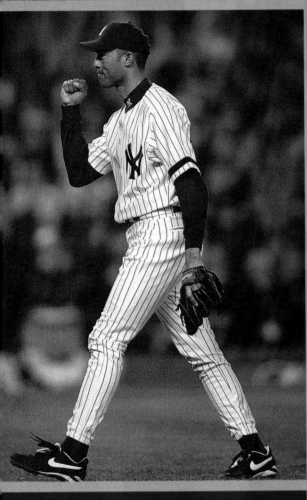

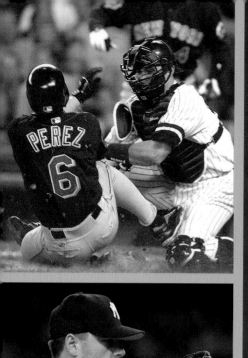

THE WORLD SERIES

Yankees 4
Mets 3

October 21
Yankee Stadium

t was a marathon of emotions, 4 hours and 51 minutes worth of intense drama played out on the biggest stage baseball could offer. When Game 1 of the 2000 Subway Series came to an end at 1:04 a.m. at Yankee Stadium, a city divided gasped for breath and hunkered down for its own version of a civil war.

What New Yorkers digested with their morning breakfast was a 4-3 Yankees victory over the Mets—a 12-inning battle that was decided on a two-out, bases-loaded single by second baseman Jose Vizcaino. This unlikely hero, a starter only because of his career success against Mets starter Al Leiter, hit an opposite-field drive to left off Turk Wendell to end the longest World Series game in history and give the Yankees their record 13th consecutive Fall Classic win.

"I was thinking I would be going to the World Series, but I didn't think I'd be the hero in the first game," said Vizcaino, a former Mets utility infielder who justified manager Joe Torre's faith by collecting four hits in the opener.

"What can you say about Vizcaino?"

Former Met Jose Vizcaino delivered the deciding blow, a 12th-inning single that scored Tino Martinez.

Torre said. "I kissed him on the cheek after the game and said, 'Thanks for making me look smart.' "

That was the kiss of death for Mets fans, who had been relishing the idea of taking down the Yankees dynasty since the playoffs opened with a Division Series victory over the San Francisco Giants. All of New York had braced for a knock-down-dragout battle, hyped unmercifully by the hungry media as the biggest baseball event since the last Subway Series (Dodgers vs. Yankees) in 1956.

Intensity was high and loyalties were divided as 55,913 fans screamed their feelings during pregame ceremonies and continued relentlessly throughout a Series opener that left the city emotionally drained.

"It was great for the fans, it was great for the players," said Mets catcher Todd Pratt.

For five innings, it was great for Leiter and Yankees lefthander Andy Pettitte, who were locked in a scoreless duel. Then all hell broke loose in a wild and crazy sixth.

Mets right fielder Timo Perez, stationed on first with two out in the top of the inning, watched first baseman Todd Zeile line a Pettitte pitch toward the left field corner—an apparent home run. Perez certainly thought so and watched the ball bounce off the top padding of the 7-foot, 5-inch fence before he began running at full speed. David Justice retrieved the ball quickly and relayed to shortstop Derek Jeter, who cut down Perez at the plate.

"We needed Jeffrey Maier," said Zeile, referring to Game 1 of the 1996 ALCS when the young Yankee fan reached over the fence to catch a similar ball that helped the Yanks record a controversial victory over his Baltimore

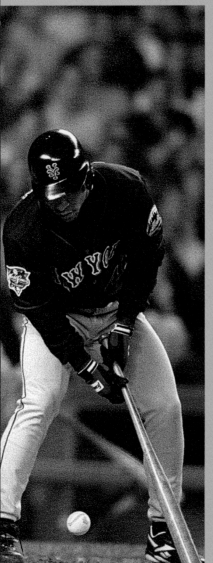

Amid the backdrop of the Subway Series, amid the dignitaries such as Spike Lee, Yogi Berra and Don Larsen, there was baseball. Andy Pettitte, the Yankees' Game 1 starter, and the rest of the Yankees staff kept Mets sparkplug Timo Perez at bay, holding Perez to a 1-for-6 performance.

Orioles. "Where was he when we needed him?"

"I thought when (Zeile) hit it, it was a home run," Torre said.

The fans were still buzzing when the Yankees struck in the bottom of the inning, Justice driving home Jeter and Knoblauch with a double into the left-center field alley. But the Mets, trying to become only the second wild-card team to win a World Series, wouldn't die.

Pettitte got into seventh-inning trouble when Benny Agbayani and Jay Payton stroked one-out singles and catcher Todd Pratt walked to fill the bases. Pinch hitter Bubba Trammell, a 7-for-18 batter in his career against Pettitte, lined a two-run single to left, and second baseman Edgardo Alfonzo gave the Mets a 3-2 lead moments later with an infield single.

"I'd like to believe we find a way to win," Torre said. And the Yankees did just that, rallying on Chuck Knoblauch's sacrifice fly to tie the game in the ninth inning off Mets closer Armando Benitez.

Extra innings belonged to the Yankees. As Mets reliever Glendon Rusch defused several threats, Yankees relievers Mariano Rivera and Mike Stanton retired the final 11 Mets they faced. The veteran Yanks finally broke through against Wendell in the 12th when Tino Martinez singled with one out, Jorge Posada doubled and Paul O'Neill was walked intentionally. Wendell retired Luis Sojo on a foul pop, but Vizcaino settled matters on the game's 396th pitch.

"We came in with very little World Series experience and got a lot of it in one night," said Mets manager Bobby Valentine, a first-time Fall Classic participant.

After his only hit of the game, Timo Perez was thrown out at the plate after Todd Zeile hit a ball off the top of the outfield wall.

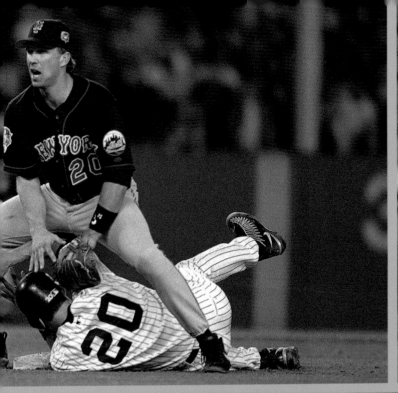

The heart of the Yankees' order produced in Game 1: David Justice (below) was 1-for-4 with 2 RBIs, Jorge Posada (lower right) was 1-for-5 and Tino Martinez (upper right) was 2-for-6. But it was Chuck Knoblauch's sacrifice fly in the ninth off Mets closer Armando Benitez (right) that sent the game into extra innings, where Jose Vizcaino's hit sent the Yankees into celebration (left).

Yankees 6
Mets 5

October 22
Yankee Stadium

Roger Clemens flinched, protecting his leg from the splintered bat that had unexpectedly sailed his way. Then he reached down, picked up the jagged piece and made the biggest pitch of his career—the one that, unfortunately, might someday define his Hall of Fame career.

"There was no intent," Clemens told reporters after the Yankees had defeated the Mets in Game 2 of the Subway Series at Yankee Stadium. "I was fired up and emotional and flung the bat toward the on-deck circle where the batboy was. I had no idea that Mike was running."

Roger Clemens was emotional on the mound all night for the Yankees; his counterpart, Mike Hampton, struggled early. Hampton gave up two runs in the first inning, including a Tino Martinez hit that scored David Justice.

117

Clemens was defending a temperamental first-inning outburst that virtually assured the remainder of the Series would be played with a mean streak. "The Play" was quickly locked into baseball's World Series memory bank, right there with images of Bill Mazeroski, Don Larsen, Reggie Jackson and Joe Carter. There's Clemens, fielding the barrel of Mike Piazza's shattered bat and firing it angrily toward the sideline, barely missing Piazza as he trots toward first base on a foul ball.

"When he threw the bat, I basically walked out and kept asking him what his problem was," said Piazza, who was kept away from Clemens by home plate umpire Charlie Reliford as players from both dugouts and bullpens ran onto the field. "He really had no response. I was trying to figure out whether it was intentional or not. ... I was

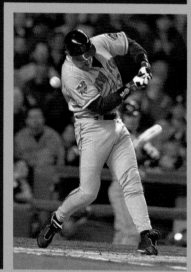

A firestorm almost erupted in the opening inning. After Mike Piazza fouled off a pitch and broke his bat, Roger Clemens fielded a jagged piece and hurled it toward the on-deck circle, narrowly missing Piazza as he ran down the first-base line.

119

Scott Brosius' second-inning homer staked the Yankees to a 3-0 lead. Paul O'Neill, who had struggled for much of the postseason, had a 3-for-4 night with two singles, a double and an RBI. The Mets had been frustrated all night by Yankees pitching and fielding. It wasn't until the bottom of the ninth inning that the Mets would score. ...

... Mike Piazza had a two-run home run and a three-run homer by Jay Payton brought the Mets within a run.

more shocked and confused than anything."

Lost in the glare of the shocking outburst were Clemens' eight innings of pitching domination, a spirited ninth-inning Mets rally that fell just short of historic and the Yankees' record 14th straight World Series victory. All anybody wanted to talk about was the first-inning incident, which occurred after Clemens had retired Timo Perez and Edgardo Alfonzo.

"I felt that (Clemens) should have got tossed," Mets pitcher Rick Reed said. "There's no room in this game for what he did." But Ed Montague, the umpire crew chief, disagreed.

"He (Clemens) just picked up the bat and winged it," Montague said. "It was just an emotional deal that built up over the months."

Driving the hard feelings were memories of a midseason interleague game during which a Clemens fastball hit Piazza on the head, sidelining him for several days. The Mets fired accusations that the big righthander had hit him intentionally, a notion that Clemens and Yankees fans dismissed as nonsense. The Mets pointed out that Piazza was 7-for-12 with three career home runs against the five-time A.L. Cy Young winner before the beaning.

When the Subway Series became a reality, talk focused on the so-called Clemens-Piazza feud and what would happen the first time they faced off. It didn't take long to find out.

"I think he knew what he was doing all along and is coming up with excuses," Mets reliever John Franco said.

"It was just so bizarre," Piazza added.

The incident only seemed to rev up Clemens, who dispatched the Mets in machine-like fashion with a 97 mph fastball and impeccable control. He cruised through eight innings, striking out nine and allowing only two harmless singles.

WORLD SERIES

2

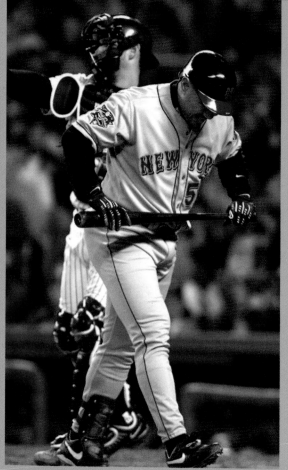

"(Clemens) was just great," Mets third baseman Robin Ventura said. "We didn't get anything going. Anytime we got somebody on base, he just shut it down."

The Yankees got to Mets starter Mike Hampton for two first-inning runs and gradually built a 6-0 lead, thanks to a Scott Brosius home run and three-hit performances by Derek Jeter, Tino Martinez and Paul O'Neill. When Clemens' back tightened up after the eighth, manager Joe Torre went to his bullpen—with near disastrous results.

"The Mets showed you why they won the National League pennant," Torre said. "They just don't roll over and die. We almost squandered it but didn't. It puts us in a good position (a two-games-to-none lead), but not a guaranteed position."

The Mets rallied when Piazza hit a two-run homer off Jeff Nelson and Jay Payton hit a two-out, three-run homer off Mariano Rivera. But Rivera struck out Kurt Abbott to end the game—one that will be remembered more for the first-inning flareup than the result.

"It's one of those crazy situations that seem to happen to New York teams," said Mets manager Bobby Valentine.

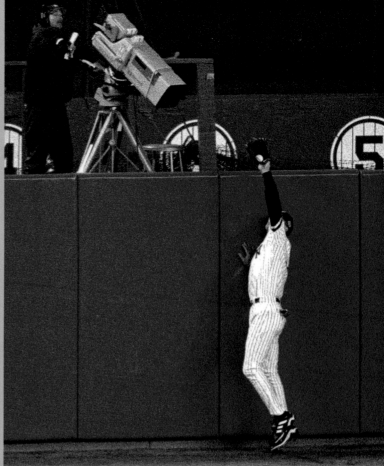

Benny Agbayani and the Mets were swinging at air in the eight innings Roger Clemens was pitching. Some good defense allowed the Mets to keep the game close in the early going. Chuck Knoblauch was tagged out trying to score in the third. Jay Payton would make a diving catch in center field. But the Yankees would have some good defense of their own. Clay Bellinger made a spectacular catch in left field to rob Todd Zeile of a home run in the ninth. Mariano Rivera actually gave up three runs in the ninth inning after Jeff Nelson was pulled.

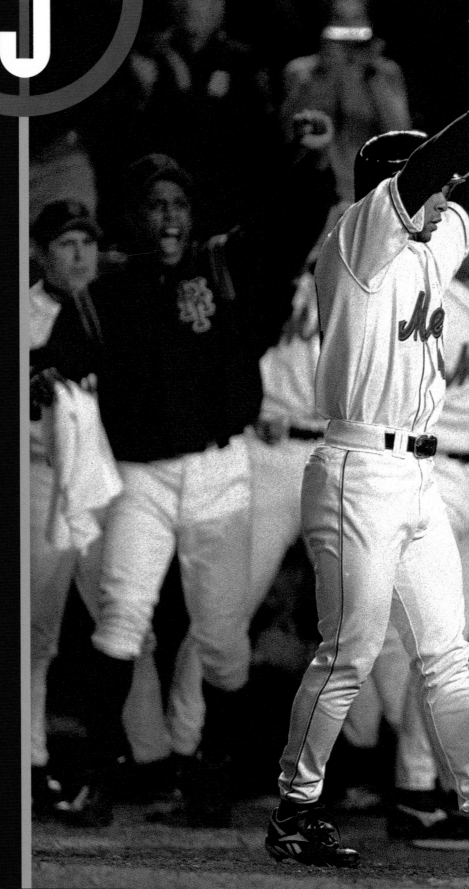

Mets 4
Yankees 2

October 24
Shea Stadium

The tension hung over Shea Stadium like a thick fog. Bobby Valentine could feel it ripping at his heart. So could John Franco, Armando Benitez and every other Mets player. As 55,299 fans gasped and roared, as New York City braced in anticipation, 14 years of frustration finally ended with a popup rather than a bang.

"These games are so intense," said Mets 40-year-old setup man Franco, who earned his first career World Series victory. "In the ninth inning, I couldn't even watch."

The win carried plenty of significance. It was the franchise's first in the fall classic since 1986, when the Mets defeated Boston in a memorable seven-game set. It was their first in this Subway Series, after the hated Yankees had prevailed in Games 1 and 2. It ended the Bronx Bombers' World Series winning streak at 14 games and it handed Orlando Hernandez, the Yanks' talented Cuban righthander, his first postseason loss after eight consecutive wins.

Todd Zeile scored the go-ahead run when Benny Agbayani doubled in the bottom of the eighth.

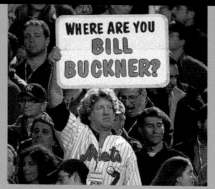

"I mean, that's all we heard was how (Hernandez has) won so many games in the postseason," said left fielder Benny Agbayani, who delivered the game-deciding hit in the eighth inning. "He never lost. So there's always a first for anyone."

Hernandez, who entered the game with flu-like symptoms, did not fall quietly. He struck out the side in the first and second innings, surrendering only a solo home run to Robin Ventura. After the Yankees had moved ahead with single runs in the third and fourth off Mets righthander Rick Reed, he worked his way through several difficult jams.

The sixth inning was vintage El Duque. Mike Piazza led off with a double and Ventura drew a full-count walk. After Todd Zeile had missed a bunt attempt, he doubled to left, tying the score and moving Ventura to third. The crowd roared in anticipation when Agbayani drew a bases-loading walk.

"It was typical El Duque," said Yankees manager Joe Torre, who watched Hernandez squirm out of that jam by striking out Jay Payton and Mike Bordick before getting pinch hitter Darryl Hamilton on a grounder. "He's up on that high wire all the time. You don't think he'll be able to get down. His determination is tough to match when it comes to big games."

Hernandez's masterful escape figured to demoralize the Mets, who went quietly in the seventh. Torre considered taking out his starter after 121 pitches, but Hernandez insisted he could go. "He was very animated and felt very good," Torre said.

Hernandez seemed to justify the

One fan was hoping to rekindle some of the magic from the 1986 World Series Champion New York Mets. Robin Ventura gave the Mets an early lead, hitting a second inning home run off of Yankees starter Orlando Hernandez, who lost for the first time in his postseason career.

decision by fanning Ventura to start the eighth—his 12th strikeout of the game—but the Mets suddenly came back to life. Zeile singled and Agbayani drove a double into the left-center field gap, giving his team a 3-2 advantage. Pinch runner Joe McEwing scored moments later on pinch hitter Bubba Trammell's sacrifice fly and the Mets were three outs away from a must win.

"We knew we couldn't go down 3-0," Franco said. "I was just in the right place at the right time."

Franco, who had worked a scoreless eighth inning, turned the game over to closer Benitez, who had failed in a Game 1 save situation. It was the combination that had gotten the Mets through a long season and it worked again for Valentine.

"We're not winning this thing without Johnny having Armando at his side," said Valentine, who squirmed a little after watching Chuck Knoblauch lead off the ninth with a single. "Johnny did his job and then it was time for Armando to do his."

After the Knoblauch scare, Benitez retired pinch hitter Luis Polonia on a fly ball to center and struck out Derek Jeter. The crowd went into a frenzy when David Justice stepped to the plate as the potential tying run. But Justice hit a harmless popup that second baseman Edgardo Alfonzo snagged for the final out.

"Our fans have been waiting 14 years for this," Franco said. "They're very loud and we just love being in this ballpark and the noise."

Zeile seconded that emotion. "A lot of people don't like to play here," he said. "The field ... there's airplanes going overhead—we feel comfortable here. It's loud."

The Mets' defense couldn't get Derek Jeter at the plate, but they got to almost everything else, including plays by Edgardo Alfonzo (above) and Mike Bordick.

After Benny Agbayani had driven in what would be the winning run on a double to left center, Joe McEwing scored an insurance run in the eighth on a sacrifice fly by Bubba Trammell. Then it was up to John Franco and Armando Benitez to shut down the Yankees.

Yankees 3
Mets 2

October 25
Shea Stadium

It was cruel reality, an in-your-face reminder that the Yankees still were baseball kings of the universe. When Derek Jeter drove Bobby J. Jones' first pitch of Game 4 over the left field wall, he took away the Mets' Game 3 momentum, quieted the 55,290 towel-waving fans at Shea Stadium and made it clear that the road to World Series success still passes through Yankee Stadium.

"I've been known to swing at the first pitch," Jeter said. "When you play games like this, you want to score early. I got a good pitch to hit and I hit it well."

The pitch was too good, said Jones, who added that "I wasn't expecting him to swing." Mets manager Bobby Valentine offered a more succinct analysis: "Putting a run on the board was the difference in the game."

If it wasn't the actual difference, it at least was the momentum-shifter after the Mets had climbed back into the Subway Series with an intense Game 3 win the previous night. The Yankees scored single runs in each of the first

The Yankees scored runs in each of first three innings, but none was as big as Derek Jeter's leadoff home run.

three innings and never trailed as they took a three-games-to-one lead and moved to within one victory of becoming the first team to win three straight championships since the 1972-74 Oakland Athletics.

"We're one win from where we want to be," said Jeter, who also tripled and scored the Yankee's final run in the third inning. Sandwiched between Jeter's big blows was a second-inning Paul O'Neill triple and Scott Brosius sacrifice fly.

When the Mets answered in the bottom of the third on Mike Piazza's two-run homer off Yankees starter Denny Neagle, the game turned into a chess match between Valentine and manager Joe Torre—an intriguing battle of the bullpens.

"When you're managing during the season, you're doing things to help you in the long run," Torre explained after several curious moves turned out well—4⅓ scoreless innings by four relievers. "When you get into a short series, you're doing things today for today."

Torre's first surprising decision came after Neagle retired the first two Mets in the fifth inning—as his lefthander was preparing to face Piazza with the bases empty. The Mets catcher had just missed a first-inning home run, pulling a drive about 10 feet foul before striking out, and he had homered in the third. Neagle was visibly upset when Torre trudged out to the mound and removed him from the game, one out short of qualifying for the victory.

"Denny was obviously disappointed when I went out there," Torre said. "I saw that look in his eye."

Neagle agreed. "When he reached for

The Mets, with Bobby J. Jones as the starter, got into quick trouble after Tom Seaver's first pitch. Jones gave up Paul O'Neill's triple to right (above, right) in the second, an opportunity the Yankees cashed in on Scott Brosius' sacrifice fly.

the ball, I was a little shocked at first," he said. "I thought we were going to discuss the situation. Obviously, I was disappointed. ..."

But righthander David Cone, a former Mets pitcher making his first appearance in the Subway Series, got Piazza, the only batter he would face, on a popup and the Yankees never looked back. Jeff Nelson worked the next 1⅓ innings, Mike Stanton retired the only two batters he faced and the ever-dependable Mariano Rivera recorded his 17th straight postseason save and record-tying sixth Series save with two shutout innings.

"It's something that if I hadn't done it (remove Neagle) and had thought about doing it and something bad had happened, I never would have been able to forgive myself for it," Torre said.

There was one negative for Torre and his Yankees—they were flooded out of their Shea Stadium locker room by a broken pipe that resulted in a visit from the New York City Fire Department.

"All of a sudden, the massage room and the weight area and the hot tub area, it was like Niagara Falls," said Nelson, who received credit for the victory. "The ceiling collapsed, there was water everywhere. This green, gunky water."

On a green, gunky night for Mets fans.

Mike Piazza homered in the third off of Yankees starter Denny Neagle. The next time Piazza came up, in the fifth, manager Joe Torre brought former Met David Cone in, and he got Piazza on a popup to second.

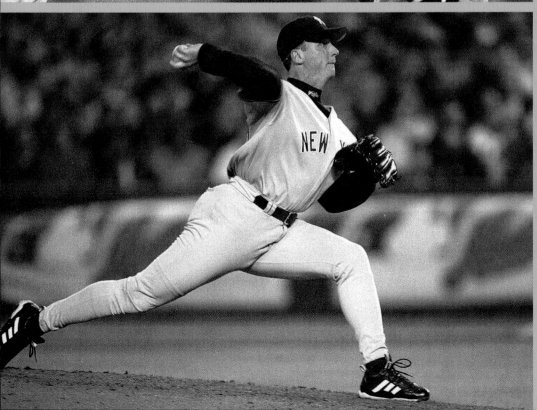

WORLD SERIES

4

Derek Jeter had another huge game, hitting a home run, a triple and scoring two runs. Then it was Mariano Rivera time, getting Jay Payton for the second out of the ninth, on his way to a perfect inning and another Yankees victory.

Yankees 4
Mets 2

October 26
Shea Stadium

He was always lurking in the background, a stocky little man whose big smile added personality to one of the greatest baseball machines ever assembled. Now Luis Sojo is a World Series hero, a card-carrying member of a Yankees club that includes such high-profile names as Babe Ruth, Lou Gehrig, Joe DiMaggio, Mickey Mantle, Yogi Berra and Billy Martin.

There was nothing exceptional about the swing Sojo layed on Al Leiter's 142nd pitch in the ninth inning of Game 5, or the ground ball that dribbled through the middle of the Shea Stadium infield, but the result was spectacular—a Yankees' victory over the crosstown-rival Mets in the much-hyped Subway Series; the Bronx Bombers' third straight championship, a feat accomplished by only three other teams, and fourth in five years; their 26th World Series title, and recognition from the rest of the baseball world for their sustained excellence.

On Luis Sojo's groundball single up the middle, Jorge Posada scored the Series-clinching run by just beating the throw to the plate. The ball bounced away from Mike Piazza on the play, and a second run scored as well.

WORLD SERIES

5

"It's the happiest day of my life," said Sojo, who became one of 10 Yankees to play on all four of the title teams. "I don't know how to explain this moment. It's a dream come true."

Sojo's timely hit broke up an outstanding pitching duel between the hard-luck Leiter and Yankees lefthander Andy Pettitte. With the game tied 2-2 and the wild-card Mets needing a win to stay alive, Leiter carried a five-hitter into the ninth inning amid speculation that manager Bobby Valentine might go to his bullpen.

"I thought he was in control," Valentine said. "He said he felt good after the eighth. It was Al's game."

Leiter made Valentine look good as he struck out Tino Martinez and Paul O'Neill to open the inning. He made several good pitches to Jorge Posada, but the Yankees catcher fouled off three two-strike offerings and finally drew a walk. When Scott Brosius lined a 1-1 pitch into left field for a single, Mets fans began fidgeting restlessly in their seats.

"I just wasn't able to close it out and finish the inning," Leiter said. "It's amazing how three hours of hard work was destroyed in a couple of minutes."

Sojo slapped Leiter's first pitch up the middle, just out of the reach of shortstop Kurt Abbott and second baseman Edgardo Alfonzo. Center fielder Jay Payton sprinted in and made a strong throw to the plate tying to get Posada, but the ball hit the runner's leg and bounced into the Mets' dugout, allowing Brosius to score as well.

When closer Mariano Rivera retired Mike Piazza on a deep fly ball with a

The Yankees got to Mets starter Al Leiter for two home runs. Bernie Williams' second-inning homer had given the Yankees a 1-0 lead; Derek Jeter's sixth-inning homer tied the game, 2-2.

WORLD SERIES

5

Andy Pettitte came up big in the decisive game, slipping only on an error in the second that allowed Al Leiter to reach first and a run to score. The Mets added another later in the inning to take a 2-1 lead.

man on base in the bottom of the ninth, the Yankees claimed the 12th win in their last 13 World Series games, reflecting sweeps over the San Diego Padres and Atlanta Braves in 1998 and '99.

"This was super satisfying," Yankees manager Joe Torre said. "It's never easy, but we had a lot of trouble putting things together this year."

The Yankees, looking old and tired, lost 15 of their last 18 regular-season games and ended the year on a seven-game losing streak. They lost the opener in both their Division Series against Oakland and their ALCS against Seattle and were extended by both teams. Pre-Series talk centered around the makeup of the 2001 Yankees, which is sure to change drastically.

"Whether you like us or not, we're winners," right fielder Paul O'Neill said. "Everybody was ready for the collapse. Everybody was waiting for us to lose."

A big spark was provided by Series MVP Derek Jeter, who continued his hot hitting with a sixth-inning home run off Leiter. Jeter's blast tied the game; center fielder Bernie Williams had given the Yankees a 1-0 lead in the second with a home run, his first hit of the Series after an 0-for-15 start.

The Mets took a 2-1 lead in the bottom of the second when one run scored on Pettitte's error and another on Benny Agbayani's infield single. Pettitte worked seven innings before giving way to Mike Stanton, who earned his second win of the classic.

The irony of the evening was not lost on New York fans who watched the Yankees celebrate the victory by

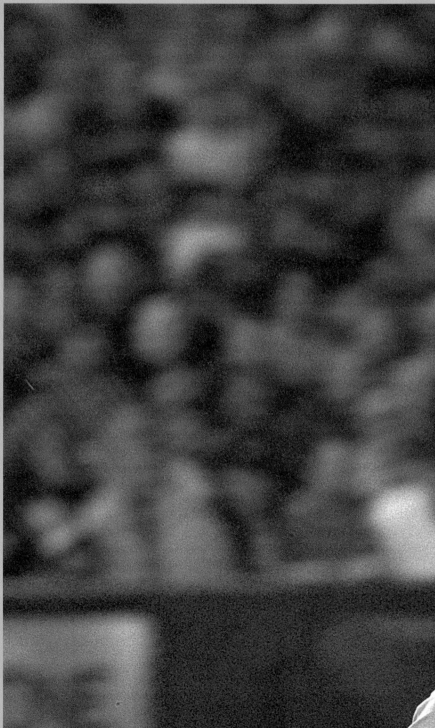

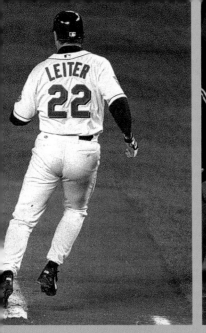

Al Leiter, Bubba Trammell and the Mets were frustrated most of the series. In the end, it was the Yankees, behind Derek Jeter's MVP performance and Joe Torre's managing, who would win the first title of the 21st century.

147

parading the World Series trophy around Shea Stadium—only a 14-minute drive from their Yankee Stadium home. When all was said and done, both teams put a gracious stamp on the first Subway Series in 44 years.

"The Mets are, in my opinion, the best team we've played in my years here," Jeter said.

"The Mets gave us everything we could want," added George Steinbrenner, pointing out that his Yankees had outscored them by only three runs. "It was great for the city of New York. I hope we don't have to go through this again for another 44 years."

Even in defeat, Valentine found a silver lining to his first World Series experience.

"This is a great group of guys," he said. "They deserve a lot of credit, but the Yankees deserve more—they're the world champions."

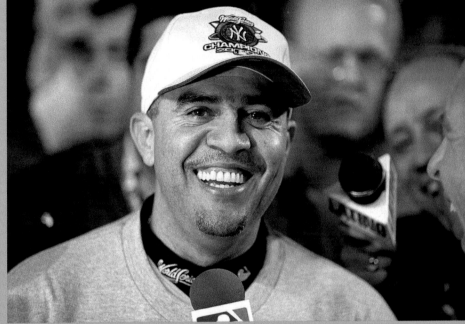